jBIO
MARKLE  Felix Rebecca

Meghan Markle

07-23-20

CHILDREN: BIOGRAPHY

CHECKERBOARD BIOGRAPHIES

MEGHAN MARKLE

REBECCA FELIX

Checkerboard
Library

An Imprint of Abdo Publishing
abdobooks.com

ABDOBOOKS.COM

Published by Abdo Publishing, a division of ABDO, PO Box 398166, Minneapolis, Minnesota 55439.
Copyright © 2020 by Abdo Consulting Group, Inc. International copyrights reserved in all countries.
No part of this book may be reproduced in any form without written permission from the publisher.
Checkerboard Library™ is a trademark and logo of Abdo Publishing.

Printed in the United States of America, North Mankato, Minnesota
052019
092019

THIS BOOK CONTAINS
RECYCLED MATERIALS

Design and Production: Mighty Media, Inc.
Editor: Megan Borgert-Spaniol
Cover Photograph: Getty Images
Interior Photographs: AP Images, pp. 9, 11, 23; Chairman of the Joint Chiefs of Staff/Wikimedia Commons,
p. 13; D. Myles Cullen/Wikimedia Commons, p. 17; Genevieve/Wikimedia Commons, p. 7; Mark Jones/Flickr,
p. 29 (top right); Shutterstock Images, pp. 5, 15, 19, 21, 25, 27, 28 (top, bottom left, bottom right), 29 (left,
bottom right)

Library of Congress Control Number: 2018966243

Publisher's Cataloging-in-Publication Data
Names: Felix, Rebecca, author.
Title: Meghan Markle / by Rebecca Felix
Description: Minneapolis, Minnesota : Abdo Publishing, 2020 | Series: Checkerboard biographies |
      Includes online resources and index.
Identifiers: ISBN 9781532119385 (lib. bdg.) | ISBN 9781532173844 (ebook)
Subjects: LCSH: Meghan, Duchess of Sussex (Meghan Markle), 1981- --Juvenile literature. | Princesses--
      Great Britain--Biography--Juvenile literature. | Television actors and actresses--United States--
      Biography--Juvenile literature. | Women entrepreneurs--Biography--Juvenile literature.
Classification: DDC 941.086092 [B]--dc23

CONTENTS

CHAPTER 1

DYNAMIC DUCHESS

Meghan Markle is best known for her role as a member of the British royal family. But before marrying a prince, Markle had achieved many accomplishments. For much of her life, she was devoted to two **passions**. These passions were acting and **advocating** for human rights.

Markle had several small roles in film and TV before becoming a star on the legal show *Suits*. This show made Markle a famous actress. But she also kept busy with her interest in human rights.

In addition to being an actress, Markle is an influential writer and public speaker. She is an advocate for women's **empowerment**. Markle has also brought attention to global issues of access to education and clean water.

In 2018, Markle earned another title. She married Britain's Prince Harry, the **Duke** of Sussex. In doing so, she became the **Duchess** of Sussex. Markle is the first **biracial** member of the modern British royal family. She is also a role model to women around the world.

Meghan Markle is known for warmly greeting her fans with a big smile and sometimes a hug.

CHAPTER 2

CALIFORNIA CHILDHOOD

Rachel Meghan Markle was born in Los Angeles, California, on August 4, 1981. She went by Meghan from a young age. Meghan's mother, Doria Ragland, was a yoga instructor and **clinical therapist**. Meghan's father, Thomas Markle, was a lighting and photography director for TV shows.

In 1988, when Meghan was six years old, her parents divorced. Meghan lived with her mother after the divorce. But she still saw her father often. Meghan also spent time with her father's two children from a previous marriage, Samantha and Thomas Jr.

> Reflecting on where I came from helps me to appreciate and balance what I have now.

When Meghan was a kid, she would visit her dad at work after school. Her dad was a lighting director on the sets of the TV shows *Married with Children* and *General Hospital.* On these sets, Meghan witnessed a world where

Thomas Markle's work gave Meghan a glimpse into the world she would later join. As an adult, Meghan would be the one acting on set and being interviewed by reporters.

companies spent millions of dollars to create shows. But this was not the only lifestyle young Meghan witnessed.

Meghan's parents wanted to give her a balanced view of the world. When Meghan was ten, Doria took her on trips to Jamaica and Mexico. On these trips, Meghan saw families that did not have a lot of money or possessions.

Meghan also witnessed poverty close to home. Both of Meghan's parents volunteered delivering meals to local families in need. They also gave food to homeless shelters. Doria and Thomas taught their daughter to be socially aware. When Meghan was 11, these values helped her stand up to injustice in a public way.

BLACK & WHITE

Meghan's mom is black, and her dad is white. **Biracial** people often experience racial **discrimination**. Meghan's parents wanted to make sure she always felt accepted. When Meghan was seven, she wanted a family set of Barbie dolls. The sets were sold with either white dolls or black dolls. Meghan's dad bought both sets and mixed them together to create a Barbie family that reflected his own.

As an adult, Markle remains close with her mother. Doria has spoken of how proud she is of Markle's many accomplishments.

CHAPTER 3

EARLY ADVOCACY

Meghan was first in the public spotlight in 1993 at age 11. Her class at school was watching a TV program when an advertisement aired. It was for dish soap made by the company Procter & Gamble (P&G). The ad said, "Women are fighting greasy pots and pans."

Meghan realized the ad sent a **negative** message. Its wording implied that only women clean in the kitchen. Meghan wanted the language in the ad to be changed. So, she wrote letters to several public figures asking for their help. One of Meghan's letters went to Linda Ellerbee. She was the host of a news show on the kids' TV channel Nickelodeon.

Ellerbee invited Meghan to appear on her Nickelodeon show to discuss her letter. Meghan's request caught the attention of P&G. Soon after, the company agreed to update its ad. P&G changed the line to, "People are fighting greasy pots and pans."

Young Meghan took part in other forms of **advocacy** too. Beginning at age 13, she volunteered at a Los Angeles soup kitchen. There, Meghan served meals to

Meghan attended Immaculate Heart High School in Los Angeles. She was her school's homecoming queen in 1998.

people in need. She volunteered at the soup kitchen until she was 17.

In 1999, Meghan graduated high school. Her next step was college, where she split her time between two areas of study.

CHAPTER 4

ACTING & ARGENTINA

For college, Markle attended Northwestern University in Evanston, Illinois. She studied both international relations and theater. International relations is the study of how politics, economics, and law are connected across the world. These topics were related to the **advocacy** and volunteer work of Markle's youth.

The time Markle had spent on TV show sets as a child influenced her interest in acting. In 2002, while still in college, Markle earned her first role on a TV show. She appeared as a guest character on an **episode** of *General Hospital*. In the following years, Markle had small roles on the shows *Cuts*, *The War at Home*, *CSI: NY*, and *90210*.

In 2003, during Markle's senior year of college, she completed an **internship** for the US **Embassy**. The internship took place in Buenos Aires, Argentina. Markle thought she would pursue a career in politics. But after returning to California, she met a manager and booked her first acting **audition**.

Markle's interests in international relations and volunteering followed her into her acting career. In 2014, she would visit US soldiers in Italy with the United Service Organizations.

CHAPTER 5

SUITS STAR

In the 2000s, Markle's acting career took center stage. In 2010, she appeared in the film *Get Him to the Greek*. The next year, she had a role in the film *Horrible Bosses*.

In September 2011, Markle married film director and producer Trevor Engelson. The couple had been dating for seven years. Also in 2011, Markle earned her biggest TV role yet. She was cast as character Rachel Zane on the TV show *Suits*. Markle played the role of a lawyer's assistant in this legal drama.

Suits was filmed in Toronto, Canada. Markle moved there for filming. She starred on the show for seven seasons, appearing in more than 100 **episodes**!

Markle's *Suits* role made her famous. She also used this job to serve others. The show regularly brought in food for

RACHEL & RACHEL

During an interview, Markle said she and her *Suits* character were very similar. They share the same first name. They are also both "ambitious, driven, and always trying to take the bull by its horns," according to Markle.

Markle poses with *Suits* costars Sarah Rafferty, Rick Hoffman, and Patrick J. Adams in 2011.

its cast and crew. Markle set up a program to deliver uneaten food to local homeless shelters.

In the following years, Markle continued to pursue her interests in both acting and **advocacy**. She would remain devoted to these pursuits throughout her life.

CHAPTER 6

BLOGGER & LEADER

Outside of filming *Suits*, Markle kept very busy in the 2010s. In a 2013 interview with *Marie Claire* magazine, she described recent trips she had taken. These included bicycling in Vietnam, camping in New Zealand, and exploring Croatia's islands and coast. In addition to her global adventures, Markle also experienced a major life change. In 2013, Markle and Engelson divorced.

In 2014, Markle began sharing her thoughts and life experiences in her lifestyle blog, *The Tig*. Markle's fame as an actress helped inspire her blog creation. She knew her fans were listening to what she had to say. She wanted to share with them ideas of value.

Markle knew many of her fans liked to read about fashion, food, beauty, and travel. She was interested in these topics too, and she wrote about them on *The Tig*. But she also wrote posts that inspired self-**empowerment** or taught readers about social issues.

The same year Markle started her blog, she also became involved in the organization One Young World.

In December 2014, Markle visited a US military base in Spain. She and other entertainers put on a holiday show for troops and their families.

One Young World gathers young leaders across the globe and encourages them to discuss and create solutions to world issues. Markle attended One Young

World gatherings in Dublin, Ireland, and Ottawa, Canada. She spoke on a **panel** discussing gender issues in global media.

In 2015, Markle's international relations work was recognized by the United Nations (UN). She was named the UN Women's **Advocate** for Women's Political Participation and Leadership. On March 8, International Women's Day, Markle gave a speech in New York City on behalf of the UN. Her speech promoted gender equality in families, marriages, politics, business, and media.

Markle's role in the public eye would increase in the coming year. But it would be for reasons far outside her advocacy work.

> It is said that girls with dreams become women with vision. May we **empower** each other to carry out such vision—because it isn't enough to simply talk about equality. One must believe in it. And it isn't enough to believe in it. One must work at it.

BIO BASICS

NAME: Meghan Markle

BIRTH: August 4, 1981, Los Angeles, California

SPOUSES: Trevor Engelson (2011-2013); Prince Harry, **Duke** of Sussex (2018-present)

CHILD: Archie

FAMOUS FOR: her acting role on the TV show *Suits*; marrying Prince Harry and becoming the **Duchess** of Sussex

ACHIEVEMENTS: acted in several films and TV shows, starring in TV show *Suits* for seven seasons; studied international relations and devoted time to several charities and organizations; became an **advocate** for UN Women and World Vision's clean water campaign

CHAPTER 7

PRINCE HARRY

In July 2016, Markle met someone who would change the rest of her life. This person was Prince Harry, a member of Britain's royal family. Harry was in Toronto to attend a sporting event. A mutual friend of Harry and Markle's set them up on a date. Markle and Harry continued to see each other after their first date.

Markle and Harry worked to keep their relationship private as it developed. After dating for a few weeks, the couple went on a camping trip to Botswana. Then they dated long-distance for months, with Markle in Toronto and Harry in England. However, they visited each other frequently.

By October, the media learned of Markle and Harry's relationship. This created a global buzz. As a famous actress, Markle had many fans interested in her personal life. Harry was also famous, but on a much larger scale.

Many people around the world are fascinated by and follow the lives of the British royal family. Nearly everywhere Harry goes, photographers and reporters

Prince Harry's brother, Prince William (*right*), married Kate Middleton (*middle*) in 2011. Before Harry met Markle, Harry's love life was a topic of public interest.

follow him to capture details of his life. The press wanted to know more about Markle and what she meant to the prince.

CHAPTER 8

MEDIA STORM & ENGAGEMENT

In November 2016, Prince Harry publicly **confirmed his relationship with Markle.** Upon this confirmation, Markle's fame skyrocketed. She became the most-Googled actress of the year!

Many people wondered if Markle and Harry would get married. This made some say **negative** things about Markle's race. Markle would be the first **biracial** person in the modern royal family. Historically, bringing a non-white individual into the family was considered a **scandal**.

Markle appeared unshaken by the public's commentary on her relationship and her increased fame. She said, "Nothing about me changed. I'm still the same person that I am, and I've never defined myself by my relationship."

Throughout the media storm surrounding her new relationship, Markle continued acting on *Suits*. She also continued her charity work, becoming a Global

Ambassador for World Vision's clean water campaign. World Vision is a large organization working globally to end poverty.

In November 2017, Markle and Harry announced that they were engaged. The news spread across the world. In December, Markle was named the most-Googled actress for the second year in a row!

CHAPTER 9

BECOMING ROYALTY

In November 2017, the British royal family announced that Markle and Prince Harry would marry the following spring. Leading up to the wedding, Markle began preparing to join the royal family. She would be busy doing charity work and attending events around the world. So, she retired from acting in preparation for this new role.

Markle's preparations also involved learning the many social rules the royal family follows. These rules are in place so royalty behave in a respectful manner with members of the public. One rule is that members of the royal family cannot post on social media. So in 2017, Markle shut down her blog. In January 2018, she closed her Facebook, Twitter, and Instagram accounts.

Markle married Harry at England's Windsor Castle on May 19, 2018. The event was televised. An estimated 1.9 billion people around the world watched it!

> With fame comes opportunity, but it also includes responsibility—to **advocate** and share, to focus less on glass slippers and more on pushing through **glass ceilings.** And, if I'm lucky enough, to inspire.

After their wedding, Markle and Prince Harry rode in a horse-drawn carriage through Windsor, England. They waved to cheering fans who lined the streets.

CHAPTER 10

ROYAL TRAILBLAZER

Markle gained more than a husband and extended family by marrying Prince Harry. She was also given the official title of **Duchess** of Sussex. Markle's role as duchess includes a variety of duties.

Charity work is an important part of royal life. Markle's work in international relations and **advocacy** made this a perfect fit for her. In her new role, Markle continues to promote gender equality and women's **empowerment**.

Markle has also brought her own individuality to the royal family. For example, royalty traditionally keep their personal beliefs private. But Markle is outspoken about being a **feminist**.

Markle's presence and **passions** have transformed the royal family. And in October 2018, she and Harry announced they would be expanding it too! In May 2019, Markle and Harry welcomed a son, Archie, to the family.

All her life, Markle has been an influential figure. She has shared her beliefs and passions as an actress, advocate, writer, and role model. And today, her impact as a trailblazing royal is felt around the world.

Markle and Prince Harry's first royal tour took place in October 2018. They visited New Zealand and other countries in the South Pacific Ocean.

TIMELINE

1981

Rachel Meghan Markle is born in Los Angeles, California, on August 4.

1999

Markle graduates high school and attends Northwestern University in Illinois. She studies international relations and theater.

2003

Markle completes an international relations internship for the US Embassy in Argentina.

1993

Eleven-year-old Markle works to have the company P&G change the language in one of its commercials.

2011

Markle earns a role as character Rachel Zane on the TV show *Suits*. She also marries film director and producer Trevor Engelson.

2013

Markle and Engelson divorce.

2016

Markle meets Prince Harry of Britain's royal family. The two begin dating.

2019

In May, Markle and Harry welcome a son named Archie.

2015

Markle is named the UN Women's Advocate for Women's Political Participation and Leadership.

2018

Markle and Harry get married on May 19. About 1.9 billion people watch the televised event around the world.

GLOSSARY

advocate—to defend or support a cause. An advocate is a person who defends or supports a cause.

audition—a trial performance showcasing personal talent as a musician, singer, dancer, or actor.

biracial—having parents from two races.

clinical therapist—a person who works with patients to identify and treat mental health problems.

confirm—to definitively state or prove true something that was previously uncertain.

discrimination (dihs-krih-muh-NAY-shuhn)—unfair treatment, often based on race, religion, or gender.

duchess—a woman of high rank in British nobility.

duke—a man of high rank in British nobility.

embassy—the residence and offices of an ambassador in a foreign country.

empowerment—a social process that helps people gain control over their own lives.

episode—one show in a television series.

feminist—one who believes that women and men should have equal rights and opportunities.

glass ceiling—an invisible barrier that prevents individuals from advancing to positions of power due to unfair judgments.

internship—a program that allows a student or graduate to gain guided practical experience in a professional field.

negative—bad or hurtful.

panel—a group of people who discuss a topic in front of an audience.

passion—something one feels very strongly about.

scandal—an action that shocks people and disgraces those connected with it.

ONLINE RESOURCES

Booklinks
NONFICTION NETWORK
FREE! ONLINE NONFICTION RESOURCES

To learn more about Meghan Markle, please visit **abdobooklinks.com** or scan this QR code. These links are routinely monitored and updated to provide the most current information available.

INDEX